Martin Luther King, Jr.

Free at Last

Martin Luther King, Jr.
Free at Last

by David A. Adler

illustrated by Robert Casilla

Holiday House / New York

IMPORTANT DATES

1929	Born January 15 in Atlanta, Georgia.
1944–1948	Studied at Morehouse College. Graduated with honors.
1947	Ordained a minister.
1948–1951	Studied at Crozer Theological Seminary. Earned Bachelor of Divinity degree.
1951–1953	Studied at Boston University. Thesis accepted and awarded doctorate in Theology in 1955.
1953	Married Coretta Scott in Marion, Georgia.
1954	Begins work as pastor of Dexter Avenue Baptist Church in Montgomery, Alabama.
1955–1956	Led boycott of Montgomery buses.
1957	Helped found the Southern Christian Leadership Conference, the SCLC. Dr. King was its first president.
1960	Moves with family to Atlanta.
1963	Led march in Birmingham, Alabama to protest racial discrimination.
1963	Gives his "I Have a Dream" speech from the steps of the Lincoln Memorial in Washington, D.C.
1964	Is awarded Nobel Peace Prize.
1965	Leads voter registration drive and march from Selma, Alabama to Montgomery, Alabama.
1966	Moves to Chicago, Illinois with family.
1968	Announces a Poor People's Campaign.
1968	Assassinated in Memphis, Tennessee on April 4.
1983	The United States Congress designates the third Monday in January as a federal holiday to honor the life and ideals of Martin Luther King, Jr.

CONTENTS

1. ATLANTA

MARTIN LUTHER KING, JR. was born in 1929, on January the fifteenth. He was born in Atlanta, Georgia.

In 1929, Atlanta was already the largest city in the southeastern part of the United States. It had an airport and fifteen railroad lines. There were factories making hundreds of products, including cottonseed oil, cotton cloth, furniture, fertilizer, and ice cream. There were more than three thousand stores in Atlanta. There were seventy-six public elementary schools. And there were *Jim Crow* laws.

Jim Crow laws separated black people from whites. They didn't go to the same schools. Blacks were kept out of certain hotels, restaurants, and railroad cars. They had to sit in the backs of buses and streetcars. Even in homes for the blind, where children could not see the color of each other's skin, black and white children were kept apart.

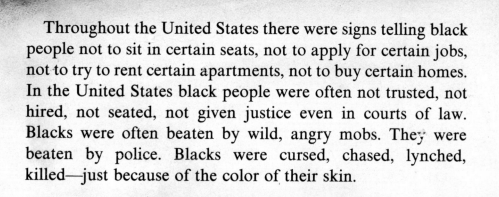

Throughout the United States there were signs telling black people not to sit in certain seats, not to apply for certain jobs, not to try to rent certain apartments, not to buy certain homes. In the United States black people were often not trusted, not hired, not seated, not given justice even in courts of law. Blacks were often beaten by wild, angry mobs. They were beaten by police. Blacks were cursed, chased, lynched, killed—just because of the color of their skin.

Clockwise, from top left: Alberta Williams King, Martin Luther King, Sr., Jenny Williams, Martin Luther King, Jr., Willie Christine King, Alfred Daniel King

Martin Luther King, Jr. liked to sing, fly a kite, ride his bicycle, and play baseball and football. He delivered newspapers and sold soft drinks from his front lawn. And he was black.

Martin's father, Martin Luther King, Sr., was the pastor of the Ebenezer Baptist Church. Martin's mother, Alberta Williams King, had been a teacher. On Sundays she played the church organ.

Martin had an older sister, Willie Christine, and a younger brother, Alfred Daniel. His grandmother, Mrs. Jenny Williams, lived with the family.

There was a grocery store near Martin's house. Young Martin played with the grocer's two sons. One day the boys were not outside, so Martin went to their house. The boys' mother told Martin that his friends would not be playing with him that day, or the next day, or ever—because they were white and Martin was black.

Martin ran home and cried.

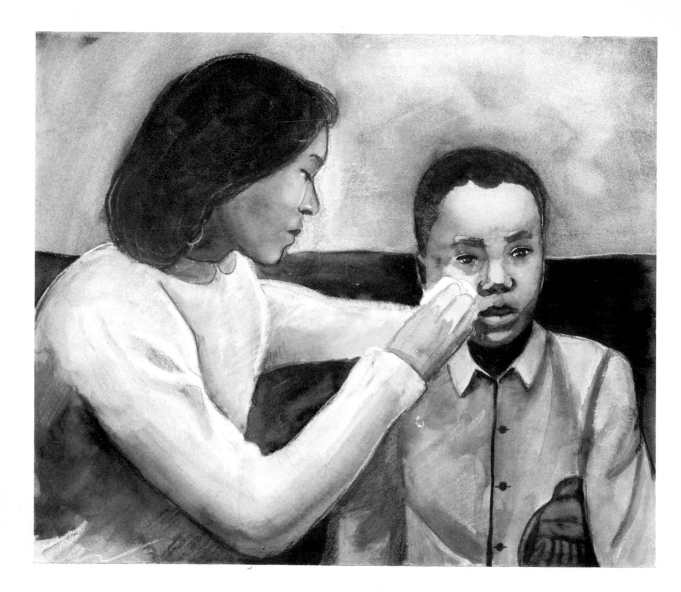

Martin's mother tried to explain to him about prejudice. She told him about the first blacks who were brought to America and sold as slaves. They were the "property" of their owners. Martin's grandfather had been a slave. Martin's mother told him about the Civil War that "freed" the slaves. But she told him the Civil War didn't end hatred and prejudice. Blacks were no longer slaves, but they weren't truly free. *Jim Crow* laws and prejudice kept blacks from being treated as the equal of whites. Then she wiped Martin's tears and told him that he was as good as anyone else.

Martin's mother taught him to read even before he started school. There were plenty of books in the King house, and Martin read many of them. He read about the lives of black heroes and heroines—Harriet Tubman, Nat Turner, George Washington Carver and Frederick Douglass. After reading those books Martin decided that to be a success in a white man's world, a black man had to be twice as smart and twice as good a Christian as everyone else.

Martin loved to listen to his father talk on Sundays from the pulpit. Martin's father had a loud, strong voice, and many times while he spoke, church members called out, "Preach, man, preach!" and "Amen!"

Words were powerful, and Martin knew it. He told his mother that one day he would use big words too.

And Martin's father was powerful. He helped get Atlanta's teachers the same pay as white teachers. He helped get the Atlanta police force to hire black policemen.

Once Martin and his father went to buy shoes. Because Martin and his father were black, the clerk told them to sit in the back of the store. "I'll sit here or I'll shop someplace else," Martin's father said.

For black people in the South buses were a special problem. Blacks had to pay the fare at the front of the bus, then run out and get in through the back door. Many times, after Martin and others paid their fares, the bus went off before they could get to the back door.

While Martin was in high school, he was a member of the debating team. For its first debate, his team had to travel by bus to another school. On the way home Martin and a friend were sitting near the front of the bus. The bus stopped and some white people got on. The driver ordered Martin and his friend to get up. They didn't. The driver cursed and threatened to call the police. Then Martin's teacher whispered and asked them to move to the back for her sake. They did.

Martin entered Morehouse College at the age of fifteen. His father had gone there. It was a black college in Atlanta.

Martin first planned to be a doctor, then a lawyer. But with the advice of his father and Dr. Benjamin Mays, the president of Morehouse, Martin decided to become a minister. The church was the center of black family life. From a church pulpit Martin felt he could reach his people and teach them about pride.

At the age of seventeen, in the Ebenezer Baptist Church, Martin gave his first sermon. He took hold of the podium and spoke out. That night Martin's father thanked God for giving him such a son.

During summers and school holidays, Martin worked in the stockroom of a mattress factory. He worked at a shipping company loading and unloading trains and trucks, and at a post office sorting mail.

One summer he worked with some friends on a Connecticut farm picking tobacco. In Connecticut, a northern state, Martin didn't see any "whites only" signs. But at the end of the summer, as the train on which Martin was riding crossed into the South, the signs went up again. Martin was told where to sit and where to eat.

At eighteen Martin was ordained a minister. A year later he graduated from Morehouse College, but he wasn't ready to begin his life's work as a pastor.

2. "UP NORTH"

After Martin graduated from Morehouse, he studied at Crozer Theological Seminary in Chester, Pennsylvania. For the first time, Martin was in a school with white students.

While at Crozer, Martin heard a lecture about Mohandas Gandhi. Martin already knew about Gandhi, but after that lecture he wanted to know more.

Gandhi had lived in India, a large country that had been ruled by the British. For almost thirty years Gandhi fought against their rule. But he and his followers fought without using their fists or guns. Gandhi was often jailed. But he believed that if the cause was good, it was an honor to be jailed. The British once fired on an unarmed crowd of Indians protesting against British rule. Four hundred were killed. But still, Gandhi called for nonviolent protest. He refused to eat for many days. His followers stopped traffic by lying across main roads. Gandhi and hundreds of followers marched two hundred miles to the sea to protest a British law they felt was unjust. And in 1947, without violence, they won their freedom from the British.

Mohandas Gandhi

Martin graduated from Crozer in 1951 at the top of his class with an *A* average.

In the fall of 1951, Martin entered Boston University to study for his doctorate in theology. And in February, 1952, Martin met Coretta Scott.

Coretta was a smart young woman with a beautiful voice. She was studying music at the New England Conservatory of Music.

Coretta was born in Marion, Alabama. She, too, knew what it meant to be a black living in the South. One day while she was at school her house burned to the ground. The police refused to look into how the fire started. Some years later her father built a sawmill and a white man offered to buy it. But Coretta's father didn't want to sell. Within a few days it too was set on fire and burned to the ground.

Martin and Coretta went to movies, concerts, and operas together. They met for lunch. They talked and talked. They were in love.

In June, 1953, Martin and Coretta were married in Alabama, on the front lawn of the Scott's house.

After Martin and Coretta completed their studies in Boston, Martin had many job offers. He could be a college teacher or a college dean. He could work in Atlanta with his father at the Ebenezer Baptist Church. He could work "up North" as a pastor in New York or Boston. But Martin decided to work "down South" as the pastor of the Dexter Avenue Baptist Church in Montgomery, Alabama.

3. MONTGOMERY

Montgomery was the first capital of the Confederate states, the southern states that fought against the North in the Civil War. It is the capital of Alabama. There were plenty of *Jim Crow* laws in Montgomery, and there were plenty of police to make sure the laws were obeyed.

Martin and Coretta first went to Montgomery in 1954. Later that year the United States Supreme Court ruled that separate public schools for whites and blacks was unfair, unequal and from then on would be against the law. That was the beginning of the end of old *Jim Crow*.

The next year, in December, a black woman named Rosa Parks was sitting in a Montgomery bus. She was sitting in the middle of the bus, just behind the "whites only" section. At every stop people got on, blacks and whites. Soon every seat was taken. The driver told Rosa and three other black riders to get up and move to the back so white riders could sit. The three other riders gave up their seats. Rosa Parks refused.

The driver pulled on the emergency brake and left the bus. He came back with a policeman. Rosa Parks was arrested.

23

Reverend Ralph Abernathy and Martin Luther King, Jr.

The next morning Mr. E. D. Nixon, a railroad worker and civil rights activist, called Dr. King. He asked if Dr. King would help organize a one-day boycott of the Montgomery buses. Blacks throughout the city would be asked to walk to work, ride by car, or take a taxi, but not to ride on a bus.

The Kings' first child, Yolanda, had just been born. It was a busy time for them. But Dr. King said he'd help.

Martin's friend, Reverend Ralph Abernathy was on the boycott committee, too. Through the coming years they would be together on many committees working for the civil rights of blacks.

The one-day boycott was set for Monday, December 5. On the Sunday before the boycott Dr. King and ministers throughout the city spoke to their congregations and told them about Rosa Parks, and asked them not to ride the buses. Dr. King helped print and distribute thousands of leaflets.

At six o'clock Monday morning Coretta called, "Martin, come quickly!"

Martin put down his cup of coffee and ran to the livingroom window. A bus was passing by. It was empty.

Martin and Coretta waited. The next bus was empty. And the next bus, too. Throughout Montgomery blacks refused to ride the buses.

That afternoon a name was given to the committee which organized the boycott. It was called the Montgomery Improvement Association, and a president was chosen, Dr. Martin Luther King, Jr.

That evening Dr. King spoke in a church filled with people and to four thousand more standing outside. "There comes a time when people get tired of being kicked about," he said.

The boycott would not end after just one day. It would go
on until blacks were promised better treatment on the buses
and until black bus drivers were hired.

Car pools were organized. The churches bought station
wagons to take people to and from work. Taxi drivers no
longer carried just one person at a time. They carried groups
of people throughout the city. Still, thousands of people had
to walk.

Dr. King and others who had done nothing wrong were arrested. Many white people in Montgomery tried to break the
boycott. They spread rumors that it had ended, that Dr. King
used the association's money to buy himself a Cadillac. It was
all untrue.

Then one night, while Martin Luther King, Jr. was at a meeting, someone threw a bomb into his home.

Dr. King was driven home. An angry crowd had gathered outside—police carrying guns and blacks carrying sticks, broken bottles and guns. Martin rushed past everyone to see if Coretta and his baby were safe. They were.

Martin went outside and told the angry crowd, "If you have weapons, take them home. . . . We must meet violence with nonviolence. . . . We must love our white brothers. . . . We must meet hate with love."

He was preaching what he had learned from Mohandas Gandhi. He was preaching nonviolence.

Almost a year after Rosa Parks refused to give up her seat, the United States Supreme Court ruled that *Jim Crow* laws forcing blacks to get on buses through the back door and to give up their seats were against United States law.

The boycott would soon end, but Dr. King knew that when blacks returned to the buses there might be trouble. "If cursed," he warned, "do not curse back. If pushed, do not push back. If struck, do not strike back."

At six o'clock in the morning, December 21, 1956, Dr. King got on a Montgomery bus. The white driver smiled and said, "We are glad to have you this morning."

Blacks riding buses no longer had to pay in the front and get in through the back. But there was still more to be done.

Dr. King wrote *Stride Toward Freedom,* a book about the Montgomery bus boycott. He traveled to talk about the book and to autograph it. He was in a New York City department store autographing when a black woman asked if he was Dr. King. "Yes," he told her. The woman quickly took something from her purse, a letter opener with a long metal blade. And with it she stabbed Dr. King.

He was rushed to the hospital. It was a serious injury. The blade of the letter opener went very close to his heart. Any quick movement, a cough or a sneeze, could have killed him.

After the three-hour operation, Dr. King wasn't angry at the woman who stabbed him. He asked that she not be jailed. He wanted her to get help. She was examined by doctors and taken to a mental hospital.

Dr. King and other black leaders formed the Southern Christian Leadership Conference, the SCLC to fight *Jim Crow* laws. Its offices were in Atlanta, Georgia. Dr. King was its president.

Dr. King spoke all over the United States. He wanted unfair laws changed. He worked to get blacks to register and vote. He was kept busy traveling to the SCLC office in Atlanta and then back to his church in Montgomery.

Then, early in 1960, Dr. King left his position as pastor of the Dexter Avenue Baptist Church and returned to work in his father's church in Atlanta as assistant pastor. By working as his father's assistant, he would have more time for the SCLC, more time to work for the civil rights of blacks throughout the country.

33

4. ATLANTA AGAIN

Throughout the South there were lunch counters where blacks were not allowed to sit. In Greensboro, North Carolina, in February, 1960, a few black students sat at one of those counters and asked to be served. The waiter refused. The students sat and waited. And they came back the next day to wait again. They were joined by other students, black and white. Soon there were sit-ins at lunch counters throughout the South. Dr. King joined a sit-in at a lunch counter in Atlanta.

Then, in 1961, came the "Freedom Rides." Black and white people rode buses through the South. They stopped to sit-in at "whites only" lunch counters, to wait in "whites only" waiting rooms of bus stations, and to use "whites only" restrooms. The Freedom Rides were organized by the SCLC, along with other groups.

The first stops were peaceful, but the peace didn't last. In Rock Hill, South Carolina, three Freedom Riders, one black and two whites, were punched, kicked and beaten. In Anniston, Alabama, an angry group of white men carrying wood clubs smashed the windows of one bus and threw a fire bomb inside. When the Freedom Riders ran out, they were beaten. In Montgomery, Alabama, a huge angry mob waited for the buses. There were reporters and photographers, but there were no police. The Freedom Riders were beaten again. When the police did come, they wouldn't arrest any of the attackers. They wouldn't even call an ambulance to help the injured.

On the night of the Montgomery beatings, Dr. King was in a nearby church. As an angry white mob gathered outside, Dr. King spoke about freedom. And through the night the people in the church sang, "We shall overcome someday." The next morning Attorney General Robert Kennedy sent United States soldiers to Montgomery to help the people leave the church without being hurt.

In 1963, Dr. King led a march for freedom in Birmingham, Alabama. Police turned powerful hoses and police dogs on the marchers. When young children marched, the police attacked them, too. Dr. King and thousands of others were jailed. But *Jim Crow* lost in Birmingham. For blacks and whites there would no longer be separate lunch counters, restrooms, and water fountains. And Birmingham businessmen would begin to hire blacks.

41

There were hundreds of other boycotts and marches for freedom. On August 28, 1963, there was the biggest march of all, the March on Washington. Two hundred thousand people, blacks and whites, joined that march. It was a happy crowd, and Dr. King spoke to them from the steps of the Lincoln Memorial.

"I have a dream," he said, "that one day on the red hills of Georgia the sons of former slaves and the sons of former slave owners will be able to sit down together at the table of brotherhood.

"I have a dream that my four children will one day live in a nation where they will not be judged by the color of their skin but by the content of their character.

"I have a dream today."

In 1963, Dr. King was chosen Man of the Year by *Time* magazine. And in 1964, Dr. King won the Nobel Peace Prize, a great honor. He was the youngest winner of the prize. Along with the Nobel Prize came a large sum of money. Dr. King gave the money to charity, to groups working to gain for blacks equal rights in America.

Dr. King led a protest in Selma, Alabama, and then a fifty-mile march of blacks and whites from Selma to Montgomery so that blacks would be allowed to register and vote.

Dr. King met with Presidents Eisenhower, Kennedy and Johnson. President Johnson helped push civil rights acts and the Voting Rights Act of 1965 through Congress. "Whites only" signs were against the law now. Blacks were guaranteed their rights in schools, factories, department stores, restaurants, hotels, movie theaters, playgrounds and in voting booths.

Dr. King preached love and nonviolence. But there *was* violence. Freedom workers, blacks and whites, were beaten and killed. And there were riots. In the 1960s, blacks were smashing, burning, and robbing the cities they lived in. The movement for blacks' rights and freedom was no longer following Martin Luther King's peaceful lead.

In 1966, Dr. King, his family, and the SCLC moved up North to Chicago. There were no *Jim Crow* laws up North, but there was poverty.

Dr. King planned a march of poor blacks, whites, Indians, Mexicans, and Puerto Ricans—a Poor People's March on Washington. In April, 1968, a few days before the march, Dr. King went to Memphis, Tennessee. He stood on the balcony of his motel on the evening of April 4. The next day he would protest with garbage workers for equal pay for blacks and whites.

But while Dr. King stood on that balcony, another man, James Earl Ray, stood in an empty bathtub in a house across from the motel. The window above the tub was open. The man pointed a rifle at Dr. King. He fired the gun. Martin Luther King, Jr. was dead.

Martin Luther King, Jr. had a dream. He dreamed of a world free of hate, free of prejudice, free of violence. The marker on his grave reads, "I'm free at last."

Martin Luther King, Jr. was just thirty-nine years old when he died. He was mourned by his wife, his four children and by millions of other people, blacks and whites. He was a remarkable man, a champion of his people. He brought needed change to his country. And in the United States, on the third Monday of every January, his country celebrates the anniversary of his birth.

47

INDEX

Text copyright © 1986 by David A. Adler
Illustrations copyright © 1986 by Robert Casilla
All rights reserved
Printed in the United States of America

Library of Congress Cataloging-in-Publication Data

Adler, David A.
Martin Luther King, Jr.: free at last.

Includes index.
Summary: A biography of the Baptist minister who
worked unceasingly for his dream of a world without
hate, prejudice, or violence, and was assassinated in the attempt.
1. King, Martin Luther—Juvenile literature.
2. Afro-Americans—Biography—Juvenile literature.
3. Baptists—United States—Clergy—Biography—
Juvenile literature. 4. Afro-Americans—Civil
rights—Juvenile literature. [1. King, Martin Luther.
2. Civil rights workers. 3. Clergy. 4. Afro-Americans—
Biography] I. Casilla, Robert, ill.   II. Title.
E185.97.K5A64 1986   323.4′092′4 [B] [92]   86-4670
ISBN 0-8234-0618-0
ISBN 0-8234-0619-9 (pbk.)